DAYS OF SLAVERY
A HISTORY OF BLACK PEOPLE
IN AMERICA
1619-1863

Written by:
Stuart Kallen

Published by Abdo & Daughters, 6535 Cecilia Circle, Edina, Minnesota 55439

Library bound edition distributed by Rockbottom Books, Pentagon Tower, P.O. Box 36036, Minneapolis, Minnesota 55435

Library of Congress Number: 90-083616   ISBN: 1-56239-017-1

Cover Illustrations by: Marlene Kallen
Inside Photos by: Bettmann Archive
                         The Granger Collection

Cover Illustrations by: Marlene Kallen

Edited by: Rosemary Wallner

TABLE OF CONTENTS

AFRICA

4

CHAPTER 1
IN THE BEGINNING

Out of Africa, since ancient times, gold, silver, ivory, and slaves have been exported to the rest of the world. Since the beginning of recorded history, African slaves were taken as the prizes of war by invading armies of every color. These men and women became servants for victorious conquerers.

When the Moslems came to Africa, around the tenth century, they sold Africans by the thousands to Persia and Saudi Arabia. Slavery was also common in Asia.

Slavery is as old as civilization. Thousands of slaves, black and white, lived and worked in ancient Rome and Greece. Europeans used each other as slaves for centuries. As a matter of fact, the word "slave" comes from a time when the Slavs, or Eastern Europeans, were sold by Germans as a source of free labor in Western Europe.

Cornelius Tacitus, a Roman historian, wrote in the ninth century that the English were used as slaves by the conquering Romans. Tacitus complained that the English were "too stupid" to be used as slaves. Despite this opinion, the English were used as slaves until the eleventh century.

In spite of being slaves for centuries, the English eventually became the master slave traders of all time. Between 1620 and 1750, the English hauled four times more people out of Africa than all the other European nations combined.

Slave dealer auctioning off slaves.

Portuguese Slavers

Anthony Gonsalves and his sailors piloted their ship down the west coast of Africa. They were very daring young men to be making such a dangerous journey. The year was 1441. Gonsalves was 1,700 miles from his home in Portugal. He knew that very few Europeans had ever been to Africa.

When Gonsalves returned to Portugal, he carried with him twelve Africans that his men had captured. Two years later, Gonsalves went back to Africa. When he returned home, he brought more Africans with him. He sold these people into slavery. Very quickly, the idea of using Africans for slaves caught on in Europe.

Kidnapping Africans and bringing them to Europe was a risky business. Many Europeans thought slavery was immoral. Also, the African coast was an unexplored place where death and danger were always a heartbeat away. But the Europeans ignored any protest against slavery and learned to overcome the dangers. Soon, a steady market developed for human slaves in Europe. Hundreds of men became slave traders to fill the growing demand.

The New World

The first blacks that came to America came not as slaves but as sailors. Some historians believe that a black man accompanied Christopher Columbus on his voyage to the New World. When Vasco de Balboa discovered the Pacific Ocean in 1513, thirty black men were with him. In the early 1500's, Estevanico, a black man, explored present-day New Mexico and Arizona for Spain. Blacks were with Hernando Cortes in Peru and with the French in Canada during the sixteenth century.

By 1515, the Spanish had a foothold in the New World. The Spaniards started exporting sugar from the West Indies to Europe. When the Arawak Indians , who lived in the West Indies, refused to work, the Spaniards turned to Africa as a source of free labor. Within a few years, the Spaniards were importing hundreds of Africans to work in the sugarcane fields.

In 1620, the first black slaves were imported to America to work in the tobacco fields around Jamestown, Virginia. Tobacco was a very profitable crop. The slave trade that surrounded it was quite profitable, also. The Spanish, Portuguese, French, English, Dutch, and Danish all fought each other to dominate the slave trade.

Landing of slaves at Jamestown, Virginia.

The bitter fighting was resolved when the English became the masters of the sea in 1713.

Slavery was not new, but in past ages, slaves were more like personal servants. When the Europeans began importing slaves, they kidnapped more than 80,000 people a year. Slave trading companies like the Royal African Company were making so much money that they called the Africans "Black Gold."

Back in Africa

The Europeans tried to paint a picture of Africa as a savage and backward place. The fact is, Africa had civilizations and cities that were at least as advanced as European cities. Africans lived in sophisticated societies where they worked in leather, weaved cotton, cast iron and bronze, and grew a variety of foods. They also were artists, dancers, musicians, scholars, and teachers. Slavers hid this fact so that they could engage in their trade. Fired by dreams of great wealth, the slave traders entered in their business as if they were trading spices or silk.

To capture slaves, European slavers would fill ships with cloth, liquor, guns, gunpowder, and food. They would sail to the African coast, row ashore, and set up trading posts. They visited the chiefs of nearby tribes and presented them with gifts. The chiefs sent out assistants who would round up strangers or members of an enemy tribe. Then the unlucky captives were traded for European guns and liquor. Many times, the chiefs were forced to provide slaves to avoid becoming slaves themselves. Some chiefs became very powerful because of the guns that they obtained from the Europeans.

Sometimes a slave ship made five or six stops before it was full of human cargo. After the ships were filled, the captain loaded corn, yams, fruits, beans, coconuts, and water aboard the ship and set sail for America.

Most African slaves that came to America were from Gambia, the Gold Coast, Guinea, or Sengal. The people from Sengal were skilled craftsmen and brought a higher price. The Eboes from Calabar were rated as undesirable merchandise. Many of them committed suicide rather than become slaves.

One-Way Passage

Conditions aboard slave ships were horrible. Small sailing vessels were packed with as many as 400 slaves. Slaves cost about $25 in Africa and sold for as much as $200 in America. The more people on board, the more money the slavers made.

Slaves were chained together at the hands and ankle. Each male was crammed into a space six feet long and sixteen inches wide. Each had a three foot high space to try to sit up in. Women and children were allowed even less space. Slaves were forced to live in filth. For weeks on end, while the boat made its long journey across the ocean, sea sickness and disease took its toll on the unwilling prisoners. The shrieks of the women and the groans of the dying filled the suffocating air.

Any slave that resisted was tortured. Many chose to jump into the ocean and drown rather than live in bondage. Some records estimate that one out of every four slaves died during the passage to America. Sometimes slaves rebelled, took command of a ship, and killed the crew. But sooner or later the rebels were harshly punished and the slaving continued.

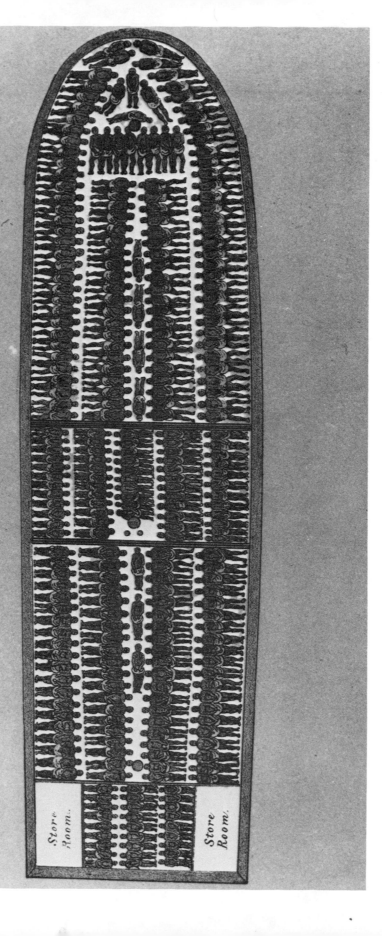

TO BE SOLD on board the Ship *Bance-Island*, on tuesday the 6th of *May* next, at *Ashley-Ferry*; a choice cargo of about 250 fine healthy

NEGROES,

just arrived from the Windward & Rice Coast. —The utmost care has already been taken, and shall be continued, to keep them free from the least danger of being infected with the SMALL-POX, no boat having been on board, and all other communication with people from *Charles-Town* prevented.

Austin, Laurens, & Appleby.

N. B. Full one Half of the above Negroes have had the SMALL-POX in their own Country.

No one knows exactly how many Africans were brought to America as slaves. Many died fighting for their freedom, millions died during the crossing, and millions more survived. Some historians say that Africa lost about 50 million human beings, or half its population, to the slave trade. While Africans died, thousands of people became wealthy from trading in human beings, including many of the so-called "good" families in Europe and America.

Strangers in a Strange Land

Once the slaves survived the ocean crossing, new ordeals awaited them in America. A town crier announced the arrival of the slave ship. Plantation owners, called planters, came down to the docks to purchase field hands and servants. The barefoot, half-naked slaves shivered in the new, cold climate as they were auctioned off.

Marriages and families meant nothing to the planters. Husbands and wives and mothers and children were torn apart and sold for the highest price. Most never saw each other again. Indeed, families would be separated on purpose so that they could not plan a rebellion. Men, women, and children cried and begged not to be separated from one another. Their cries were ignored by the slavers.

Auction sale for slaves.

Even members of the same tribe were separated. Africans have over one thousand different languages. Members of one tribe might not be able to talk to members of another tribe. Members of the same tribe had a common language, so they were separated. Africans often found themselves stranded, with no families, not knowing the language of the white people, and not being able to communicate with the other slaves. What lay ahead for the slaves was a lifetime of hard work for no pay, meager food, and the lash of the whip.

Thousands of field hands were needed to clear the forests for plantations. Thousands more were needed for planting, harvesting, and processing rice, indigo, cotton, sugar, and tobacco. By the end of the 1600's twice as many black people as white lived in America. Most of them lived in the South.

18

CHAPTER 2
LIVING IN AMERICA

"I work my slaves in a hurrying time until 12 o'clock at night," a Florida planter bragged in 1830, "then I have 'em up again by 4 in the morning." This was the life of a slave. Twenty-hour workdays were the rule, six days a week. Slaves froze in the winter, sweated in the hot summer sun, and got drenched in the rain.

A gong or horn awakened the slaves before dawn. Slave drivers marched them to the field immediately where they worked until about 10 a.m. After a meal of hoecake (cornmeal heated on a hoe over an open fire) the slaves worked until late in the afternoon. Then they took another fifteen-minute break for a meal. The work continued until it was too dark to see. Only after the crops had been turned in, the mules fed, the wood chopped, and the master attended to, did the slaves have time to mend their clothes, eat, drink some water, and relax. Men, women, and children were all worked this way. For this, they were awarded one blanket, one pair of shoes, and two changes of clothes a year.

The Cotton Gin

Tobacco was the major crop in America until the Revolutionary War in 1776. After the Americans won their independence from Great Britain, cotton became a major crop because of a new invention. In 1792, Eli Whitney, a student from Yale, invented the cotton gin. Although the cotton gin was operated by a hand crank, "gin" was short for engine. This invention separated the sticky seeds from cotton. Before the cotton gin, this work was done by hand through a long, slow process.

Before the invention of the cotton gin, a whole family, with the help of the house servants, gathered before the fireplace after dinner. Everybody removed the cotton lint from the seeds, fiber by fiber. In this manner, a few pounds of cotton could be gathered before bedtime.

With the cotton gin, a single person could seed ten times more cotton. The cotton was put in a box with opposing rakelike fingers. A crank was turned and the cotton was separated from the seeds. After a few years, larger models were made that used a horse for power. With those, fifty times more cotton could be seeded than before.

Cotton quickly became the major crop in the South. To grow cotton, pick it, gin it, and bail it was very hard work. If one man alone were to do all the work to bring one acre of cotton to market, that man would have to walk a thousand miles between the rows of cotton from spring to fall. Hundreds of thousands of acres of cotton were planted in the South, and slaves did all the work.

First cotton gin on a southern farm.

In one year, 1803, ten years after the invention of the cotton gin, more than 20,000 Africans were brought to Georgia and South Carolina to work the cotton fields. Most of them were supplied by

The Cotton Gin

New England slave traders. Whitney's gin made cotton big business. It also tightened the chains of slavery tighter than ever around the ankles of the Africans.

Life on a Plantation

Tobacco and cotton were only profitable if grown on huge areas of land. Plantations of 10,000 acres or more were common during the 1800's. Planter families lived like the kings and queens of European royalty. Their mansions were filled with Persian rugs, fine artwork, and imported furnishings. Some mansions contained a music room, a library, a ballroom, a variety of parlors, a huge dining room, a kitchen, and a wine cellar. Lavish parties were regularly given for visting friends and relatives.

Surrounding the mansion were a bake house, a stable, a dairy, a schoolhouse where a teacher lived, a blacksmith shop, a brickworks, a smokehouse, a flour mill, and cabins for slaves. Everything that could not be made on the plantation was imported from Europe.

Skilled Workers

Slaves were important for the operation of almost every aspect of the plantation. Not all slaves were field hands. Skilled craftsmen were needed to build and repair houses, barns, roads, bridges, gates, and fences. Many of these craftsmen were slaves. Slave owners could hire out their skilled slaves to other planters and collect a fee. Many slave owners encouraged their slaves to learn skills for this reason. Slaves became railroad firemen, bricklayers, blacksmiths, printers, carpenters, and more.

House servants were generally better off than field hands. Cooks, butlers, nannies, hairdressers, seamstresses, and others were used to serve planter families. Many times the house servants helped raise the children of the planter families. House servants were sometimes allowed to learn to read and write.

CHAPTER 3

BLACK CONTRIBUTIONS
TO EARLY AMERICA

Many blacks, free and slave, made names for themselves in the early days of America. Black writers, actors, athletes, inventors, and soldiers proved their skills and courage to white society again and again. Here are the stories of just a few of the most famous black people in American history:

Crispus Attucks - 1723-1770
Leader in the Revolution
"The first to defy and the first to die . . ." so read a line of poetry about Crispus Attucks. In 1770, a group of men in Boston were protesting British policies in America. Crispus Attucks, a black sailor, was the first to be shot when the British opened fire on the protesters.

Attucks was a slave in Massachusetts until he was twenty-seven years old. He ran away from his owner and went to sea on a whaling ship. For the next twenty years, Attucks sailed the world, hunting whales. While at sea, he taught himself to read and write. Attucks protected his freedom and longed for the freedom of others. It was natural for Attucks to join Americans who were fighting for their freedom from the British.

On March 5, 1770, a mob gathered in Boston Commons. British soldiers were assembled to keep the angry mob in line. When a soldier named Huge Montgomery hit a small boy on the head with his rifle butt, the angry crowd, led by Attucks, began pelting Montgomery with ice and snowballs. Twelve other soldiers came to Montgomery's aid with rifles and bayonets at ready.

Attucks charged ahead with a large stick, yelling, "Don't be afraid. Knock 'em over. They dare not fire." Attucks was wrong. The soldiers fired, killing Attucks immediately. Nine other men were wounded, four of whom died. Newspapers all over the country called the attack the Boston Massacre.

Attucks body lay in state in Boston's Faneuil Hall for three days. Thousands attended his funeral. Shopkeepers closed their stores in protest. The Boston Massacre marked the beginning of a series of events that led to the American Revolution.

Jean DuSable - 1745-1818
City Founder

Jean DuSable was born in Haiti to an African woman and a French man. When Jean was young, his father took him to France to be educated. DuSable went to New Orleans when he was older and became a fur trapper.

In 1769, DuSable stopped at a place the Native Americans called "Checagou." DuSable thought the location was a good one to set up a trading post. Checagou grew and was eventually renamed Chicago. Today it is the third largest city in America.

DuSable was successful because he could speak English, French, Spanish, and several Native American dialects. DuSable also became friends with the Native American tribes in the area and traded furs with them. Before long, DuSable's post expanded and included a horse stable, workshop, bakery, dairy, smokehouse, and other buildings. It soon became the main supply station for hundreds of fur trappers in the area.

DuSable was not honored in his lifetime, but in 1968, he was finally credited for being the founding father of Chicago.

Benjamin Banneker - 1731-1806
Inventor, Astronomer

"The color of the skin is in no way connected with the strength of the mind or intellectual powers." So spoke Benjamin Banneker a genius of incredible powers.

Benjamin Banneker was born in Baltimore, Maryland, in 1731. His mother was an English woman and his father was a slave. He was taught to read and write and showed a strong interest in math at a young age.

When Benjamin was nineteen years old, he met a traveling salesman who showed him a pocket watch. Banneker had never seen one before, and he went home and drew up plans to make one. He carved the entire watch out of wood and made each gear by hand. His homemade watch kept perfect time for forty years; it was the first watch made in America.

Banneker studied the stars, and predicted a solar eclipse on April 14, 1789. Many astronomers disagreed with him, but Banneker was right. Banneker published an almanac listing weather information, eclipses, tide tables, and the hours of sunrises and sunsets. In addition, Banneker published antislavery poems and essays.

Banneker moved to Washington, D.C., in 1791 when President George Washington asked him to help build the nation's capital. Banneker surveyed the area and helped plan the city.

When Thomas Jefferson said that blacks were not as smart as whites, Banneker wrote him a letter in protest. He included his almanac, and Jefferson quickly changed his mind. Banneker's almanac was shown in Britain's Parliament and the French Academy of Sciences in Paris. Banneker proposed that the United States government establish a Department of Peace, give free education to everybody, and eliminate the death penalty. In many ways, Banneker was a man ahead of his time.

Peter Salem - 1750-1816
Revolutionary War Soldier

Because the Declaration of Independence said, "All men are created equal," many black soldiers signed up to fight for independence.

During an early battle in the Revolutionary War, in June 1775, only 1,500 American soldiers faced over 2,500 British soldiers in the Battle of Bunker Hill. The British kept charging up the hill and the Americans kept fighting them off. When the British thought they were about to win the battle, their commander, Major John Pitcairn yelled, "The day is ours!" That was the last thing Pitcairn said, because as soon as he spoke, Peter Salem shot him in the chest and killed him. Pitcairn was one of the best British majors, and his death was a great blow to the British.

During the Revolutionary War, many whites did not want blacks to fight in the revolution. George Washington ordered all black men to leave the army. The British took advantage of Washington's order and offered freedom to any slave who joined the British Army. Washington quickly changed his mind and allowed blacks to fight. As soon as he did, Peter Salem joined the revolution.

The Battle of Bunker Hill

Many blacks thought that slavery would be abolished if the Americans won. Five thousand blacks served in the Revolutionary Army. Blacks fought in every battle of the eight-year war.

Peter Salem fought bravely at Concord, Lexington, Bunker Hill, Stoney Point, and Saratoga. But blacks were not helped much by the Revolutionary War. After the Americans won, many black soldiers were forced to become slaves again. Salem died in a poorhouse in 1816.

Paul Cuffe - 1759-1817
Shipping Merchant, Humanitarian

Paul Cuffe fought for the rights of black people in America. But Cuffe believed that blacks could only be free if they returned to Africa. He is considered the father of the Black Back-to-Africa movement.

Paul Cuffe was born on Cuttyhunk Island in Massachusetts. His father was a slave and his mother was a Wampanoag Indian. When he was sixteen years old, Cuffe decided to make his living from the ocean. Eventually, he became wealthy from shipping, fishing, and whaling. Cuffe owned ten ships that sailed to Europe, Africa, Canada, and the Caribbean.

The father of the Black Back-to-Africa movement.

Cuffe's wealth could not protect him from discrimination. The 1778 Massachusetts Constitution denied blacks and Native Americans the right to vote. Cuffe refused to pay his taxes as a result. Cuffe pointed out to the Massachusetts lawmakers that many blacks and Native Americans were fighting in the American Revolution. He said that everyone should be able to vote. The lawmakers finally agreed. In 1783, they granted the right to vote to all tax-paying blacks. When the state would not provide free education to the children in his town, Cuffe built a schoolhouse on his own farm and donated it to the city of Westport.

When the leaders of the hard-won American Revolution refused to end slavery, Cuffe looked to Africa for freedom. In 1810, Cuffe traveled to Sierra Leone, in Africa, with the idea of setting up a colony for American blacks. In 1815, Cuffe sponsored twenty black children and eighteen adults to settle with him in Africa.

At the same time that Cuffe was setting up an Afro-American colony, the American Colonization Society was formed. Its leaders were slaveholders that wanted to send free blacks back to Africa so that they would have more control over the slaves. The American Congress agreed with the slaveholders and bought territory in Africa where blacks could settle. The country was called Liberia (after the word "Liberty") and its capital was named Monrovia after President James Monroe.

Over the next thirty years, more than 14,000 black people returned to Africa. Some were free blacks, others were slaves who were freed under the condition that they return to Africa. Many blacks would not leave America because they wanted to fight for freedom for the millions of blacks living there. They believed that since blacks had built America they were entitled to the benefits that America provide to white people.

York - 1770-1832
Explorer
In 1803, President Thomas Jefferson bought 875,000 square miles of unexplored territory from France. Stretching from Canada to Mexico and from the Mississippi River to the Rocky Mountains, the Louisiana Purchase doubled the size of the United States overnight.

Since no one knew what lay in the vast territories, Congress authorized Meriwether Lewis and William Clark to explore the area. Jefferson also wanted Lewis and Clark to find a route to the Pacific Ocean.

In 1804, the Lewis and Clark expedition set out for the wilderness. Among the forty-five men and one woman in the party was a black man named York. York was the personal slave of William Clark and had been friends with him since childhood. Standing over six feet tall and weighing more than two hundred pounds, the twenty-three-year-old York was an imposing figure. York was an agile hunter and was strong and athletic. He spoke French and several Native American dialects.

The expedition was guided by a French trapper named Toussaint Charbonneau. His wife, Sacajawea or "Bird Woman" was a Shoshone Indian. When the expedition met with other Native American tribes, Sacajawea told her husband what they were saying. Carbonneau would tell York in French, and York would translate to English for William Clark. York's translations were very important to the expedition.

The Native Americans were amazed by York.
They had never seen a man of his size, skin color,
and ability. They thought his face was painted
with charcoal, which was what Native American
warriors sometimes did. The Native Americans
tried to rub the color off his face. Because they
admired him, York was assigned the task of
trading with the Native Americans for food and
horses.

York was a participant in the Lewis and Clark expedition.

The expedition reached the Pacific Ocean in November 1805. The group had crossed Montana, Idaho, Washington, Oregon, and North and South Dakota. After enduring a harsh winter in Washingtom, they returned to St. Louis, Missouri, on September 23, 1806. The members of the expedition had endured incredible hardships but they brought back important information about western America.

After the expedition, Clark freed York. York traveled to Kentucky to live with his wife who was a slave there.

Denmark Vesey - 1767-1822
Slave Revolutionary

Denmark Vesey was a lucky man. In 1799, he won 1,500 dollars in a lottery. He used 600 dollars to pay for his freedom. In 1822, he tried to gain freedom for every slave in Charleston, South Carolina. This time he paid the price with his life.

When Vesey bought his freedom from a sea captain in 1799, he set up a carpentry shop. Before long, Vesey was a wealthy man. Vesey was outspoken about the evils of slavery and in 1821 he decided to do something about it.

Vesey decided to organize a massive slave revolt that would allow blacks to take over Charleston, South Carolina. Vesey chose Gullah Jack, an African-born magic man, and several slaves belonging to the governor of South Carolina to lead his strike force. Eventually his revolution numbered 9,000 members.

Vesey planned his revolution to begin on July 14, 1822. His army would move at midnight and strike several key points in the city. Unfortunately for Vesey, a house slave betrayed his revolution. The slave told city authorities of the plan and soon Vesey was forced to run away from Charleston. The police found Vesey hiding in the woods and arrested him.

Vesey was tried and convicted. The judge handed down a death sentence. On July 2, 1822, Vesey was hanged with four other followers. Thirty-seven other blacks were put to death for their part in the revolt. Vesey gave his life trying to improve the conditions of others.

Joseph Cinque

Joseph Cinque -- 1817-1879
Captured Slave

The only English words that Joseph Cinque knew were, "Give us free, give us free." And those were the words he spoke in a New Haven, Connecticut, courtroom in 1840. His trial was the most sensational one of its day. It became a rallying, point for abolitionists trying to abolish slavery in the United States.

It all started in Lomboko, Africa, in 1839. Joseph Cinque was captured by Portuguese slave traders and put aboard a ship bound for Havana, Cuba. The conditions on the ship were so horrible that half of the slaves died during the journey. It was illegal to import new slaves to Havana, so Cinque was secretly sold to a man named Ruiz.

Cinque was put on another ship bound for the Island of Principe. Desperate to escape, Cinque pried a nail out of the ship's side and used it to unfasten the chains that bound him and the other slaves. The freed slaves snuck up on the deck and killed the captain and the crew of the slave ship. Then they captured Ruiz and his partner Montes.

The Africans did not know how to pilot a large ship, so they made Ruiz and Montes sail ship.

Cinque ordered Montes to turn the ship east so that the slaves could return to Africa. Montes tricked Cinque and turned the ship north in the middle of the night. Ruiz and Montes hoped to reach the Southern United States where slavery was legal. Instead, they sailed off course and landed in Montauk Point on Long Island, New York. When Cinque and some other Africans went ashore to find food and water, they were arrested and charged with mutiny and murder.

The Cuban government demanded that the ship and the slaves be returned to them. American abolitionists protested, saying that Montes and Ruiz were the real criminals.

Cinque's trial was held on January 7, 1840, in New Haven, Connecticut. The trial was featured in all the major newspapers. Yale law school canceled classes so that its students could attend. Although Cinque could not speak English, he argued through an interpreter that he had been kidnapped and had a right to resist by any means necessary. The court agreed, but the decision was appealed. A higher court upheld the decision and Cinque and the other Africans were allowed their freedom. But it was only temporary.

President Martin Van Buren wanted to please Southern slaveholders. Van Buren ordered the Justice Department to appeal the case once again, this time to the Supreme Court.

At this point, former President John Quincy Adams came out of retirement to represent the Africans. Adams was almost eighty years old and nearly blind, but he was still active in the antislavery movement. After arguing before the Supreme Court for eight hours, Adams won the case. On March 9, 1841, nearly two years after he had been kidnapped, Cinque was set free. He and the other Africans returned to Sierra Leone. Cinque and the others were some of the few slaves that were allowed their freedom in American courtrooms.

Garcia - 17??-1816
Soldier

In the years before Florida became a state, many slaves ran away and sought refuge there. Many runaway slaves settled among the Seminole Indian tribes. Others started small communities in the dense forests. Over 300 men, women, and children of black, Seminole, and mixed blood lived in one such settlement called Fort Negro. The fort was protected by black soldiers under the command of a man named Garcia.

Fort Negro was originally built by the British on the Apalachicola River, about sixty miles from Georgia. The British abandoned the fort after losing the War of 1812. Black settlers moved in, and the fort quickly became the symbol of freedom for slaves all over the South. Many ran away hoping to live there.

The fort was in territory owned by Spain. But southern slaveholders were concerned that the fort posed a threat to their way of life. United States General Andrew Jackson ordered the Seventh Military to destroy Fort Negro. Attacking a fort in Spanish territory was considered an invasion of a foreign country by most governments. Jackson did not care and attacked the fort anyway.

On the morning of July 27, 1816, a large United States military force surrounded Fort Negro and ordered Garcia to surrender. Garcia refused. The fort was strong and the men inside were heavily armed. The U.S. forces heated up cannonballs and fired them into the fort. One of the hot cannonballs landed in a shed full of gunpowder. That touched off an explosion that was heard for miles. The fiery blast killed or wounded 200 people inside the fort. The remaining sixty-three survivers were returned north to slavery. The brave commander Garcia was taken prisoner and shot by a firing squad.

A Final Word

The people's stories told here are just a few of the thousands, possibly millions of heros in the black struggle against slavery. No one will ever know all the acts of kindness, bravery, and strength performed by people under the horrible burden of slavery. In Africa, on the slave ships, in the markets, and on the plantations, people helped each other survive every day. If you are interested in reading more about Africa, slavery and black American heros, the information is only as far away as your local library.

INDEX